SPLASH IT!

99 CUSTOMIZABLE PRESS RELEASE TOOLS, TEXTS & LAYOUT TEMPLATES

Caroline Hurry

Copyright ©2023 by Caroline Hurry. All rights reserved. The content contained within this book may not be reproduced, duplicated, or transmitted without the author's or publisher's direct written permission available from caroline@carolinehurry.com
Website: https://carolinehurry.com

Legal Notice:

This copyright-protected book is intended only for personal use.

Disclaimer Notice:

Hey there, reader! Before we dive into the world of media texts, tools, and templates, you might notice the numbering in this book is neither predictable nor linear. All the tips, customization exercises, templates, tools, and apps add over 99 items. Feel free to wear your detective hat and count them if you like.

For formatting order, I started afresh in every chapter. The author is not responsible for any numerical confusion. Please embrace the randomness, jump in wherever you like, and start customizing.

SPLASH WHAT?

ANYTHING YOU LIKE

SPLASH IT! IS A starting point for anyone needing to promote a book, product, skill, announcement, familiarization tour, or venue.

Customizable exercises save you time and guesswork.

Level up your marketing game with free tools and insider tips. Embrace the randomness. Dip in, jumpstart your creativity, and make waves! – Caroline

Contents

Ride the Wave!   1
How To Use This Book

Before We Dive In   3
Let's Splash Out With The Basics
   The Basic Structure
   7 Visual Wizardry Keys
   7-Point Checklist
   Where To Send Your Release
   How To Use The Layout Templates

Layout Templates Overview   7

Splash It!   9
Elevate Your Brand

Share   11
A Curated Collection
   Share A Collaboration
   Share a Roadhouse Trail
   Customize Exercise

A Collaborative Template	17
Proof	19
Participation and Commitment	
10 Proof Sprinkles	
Proof of Participation	
Prove Your Philanthropy	
Customize Exercise	
Participation Template	25
Launch	27
Leave a Lasting Impression	
How To Launch a Book	
Write A Press Release	
Spark Feature Ideas Around Your Book	
Customize Exercise 1	
Customize Exercise 2	
Book Launch Template	35
Announce	37
Start Spreading the News	
Announce a Sponsored Wine Event	
Announce an In-Studio Concert	
Announce A Juice Line	
Announce a Scientific Breakthrough	
Announce an Alliance	
Announce an Anniversary	
Announce a Partnership	
Announce Job Opportunities	
Customize Exercise	

Job Opportunities Template 46

Showcase 47
Airlines and Vacation Venues
    Showcase Your Ideas
    Showcase an Airline Offering
    Showcase Tourist Operator Venues
    Customize Exercise

Airline Feature Template 53

Host 55
A Familiarization Tour
    Customize Exercise
    Hosting a Scandinavian Trip

Familiarization Tour Template 59

Introduce 61
Set Up Productive Relationships
    Introduce Yourself Or Your Brand
    An Introductory Proposal Template
    7 Key Components
    Introduce Yourself as a Photographer
    Introduce Yourself as a PR Consultant
    Introduce a Chef Executive Office
    Introduce A Product Line
    Introduce a Safari Lodge
    Introduce an Innovative Startup

Introductory Templates 70

Troubleshoot 71
Consequences of Customer Offense

    Disastrous PR Strategies
    Crisis Management
    3 Ways to Move Forward
    Rebuilding the Brand
    Damage Control Customize Exercise
    Write a Letter of Apology
    Respond to a Scathing Venue Review
    Turn Down a Proposal

Bonus Chapter   81
Hack the Art of Media Whispering
    Don't Spray and Pray
    Don't Assert Your Needs
    Don't Extend Late Invitations
    Don't Dress Puffy Marketing Fluff as News
    Don't Issue Instructions
    Don't Send Irrelevant Unsolicited Pitches
    Don't Solicit Guarantees
    Don't Call To Ask When It's 'Going In'
    Don't Express Disappointment
    Photographic Frustrations
    7 Tips To Get Noticed
    How to Woo the Media
    Six Media Matchmaking Tips
    Plant In The Soil
    Hack Media Whispering With ChatGpt

Layout Links   89
More Useful Tools   91
Afore ye go   95

About The Author

RIDE THE WAVE!

HOW TO USE THIS BOOK

Where, oh, *where* can I find work? It's a common lament from the freshly retrenched to any feisty 55 or 60-year-old who no longer fits the corporate mold.

When you're unemployable, it's time to maximize your experience. Dive into the vast pool of your unique skills and wisdom. Follow your passion. Build a client base from scratch.

But *how?*

Grab a pen and a piece of paper. Draw three columns. First, list everything you can do, from chicken sexing to mayo making. In the second, list all the things you're good at. In the third and most crucial column, what do you ENJOY doing?

Know your strengths and weaknesses. Take me, for instance. My initial chicken sexing skills led to a seven-cock-a-doodle situation that drove my neighbor's fiancé from her home; a favor, in retrospect. Of course, *now* I know it's all in the comb. Fowl incidents spark ideas for a book about suburban hen-steading.

Speaking of strengths, numbers are not on my strong list. So while there *are* more than 99 hints, tips, insider secrets, text, and layout templates inside these pages, I didn't number them from 1-99 because it complicated my DIY formatting – in case you think I strayed from the subtitle.

Okay, so back to what you *can* do. Whatever it is, you have to market it. Whether writing a press release for your local media or drafting a proposal to showcase your skills, *Splash It!* has you covered with text prompts you can adapt to suit your purposes.

Every chapter offers a customized exercise where you ask yourself a few leading questions. Who is your target market? What do you want them to know? What is your ultimate goal?

Once you've chosen a couple of local publications or blogs that would suit your product or services, look at the various options for crafting a purposeful press release and customize the text according to your unique situation.

With *Splash It*!, you can make waves, create connections, and leave a lasting impression. Embrace the art of customization, let your creativity flow, and learn to craft irresistible PR copy that hits the mark!

Before We Dive In

Let's Splash Out With The Basics

Whatever your reason for seeking publicity, a compelling press release can help you stand out. Each chapter offers customizable text templates and a layout suggestion for beginners unsure where to start.

How you approach journalists, editors, or book bloggers is almost as crucial as your media kit. The Bonus Chapter, culled from *Write, 6 Successful Self-Publishing Strategies on a Shoestring*, will help you hack the dark arts of media whispering.

There are two parts to a press release. The first, from the headline to the body, should include all essential information about your announcement. The second or boilerplate is for information about yourself or your brand.

The Basic Structure

1. **Headline** – make it short, snappy, and accurate.

2. **Subheading** – expand on the headline.

3. **Blurb** – introduce three or more of the Sacred Six key points – who, what, when, where, why, and how.

4. **Body** – provide further details about the news and quotes from relevant spokespeople or experts.

5. **Boilerplate** – provides background and contact information.

7 Visual Wizardry Keys

1. A heading or subject line that tells the story and mentions the keyword

2. Ensure there's plenty of white space to rest your eyes.

3. Professional formatting is easy to digest, with well-laid-out headlines and captions.

4. Break up the text with short, reliable paragraphs, bullet points, and bold headings.

5. Ensure sentences are short and straightforward. Essential information should command attention.

6. Number critical information for easy reading. Aim for skimmable and scannable.

7. If you have a business logo, include it in the top right-hand corner of the page.

7-Point Checklist

1. Does your blurb or introductory first paragraph summarize your story's critical points?
   Answer the Sacred Six questions

2. How does your angle or hook set your product apart?
   Offer a deal or discount if you struggle to find an angle.

3. Does your headline invite further perusal?

Try an unusual statement, bizarre statistic, or provocative question. Tantalize further with your subhead.

4. Have you considered the publication's audience?
   Tailor your release accordingly.

5. Have you provided any credible supporting quotes or statistics for additional relevance to your piece?
   Include hyperlinks to the original research.

6. Is it brief, clear, concise, engaging, and jargon-free?
   Less is more. Aim for 350 words or fewer.

7. Have you included contact details such as website and phone number?
   Explain who you are in the notes to the editor below the press release.

Where To Send Your Release

Three ways to find a relevant editor for any news or online magazine agency:

1. **Research the agency**: Find the sections related to your press release topic. Most online outlets list the editors, journalists, their beats, and contact information on their websites.

2. **Use online directories or professional networks** like LinkedIn to search for editors or journalists using keywords related to your topic.

3. **X** (formerly Twitter) is another favorite writer's hangout. It's a great place to connect with specific journalists or editors you'd like to approach. Try the hashtag #amwriting

How To Use The Layout Templates

Follow these four steps to bring your vision to life using each chapter's A4 Layout Templates for easy and enjoyable customization.

1: When you click on the link for each template, it will take you to Canva. Sign up for a free account with this user-friendly graphic design platform. Registration is quick and easy.

2: Open up the template, then replace the headlines, descriptions, dates, or other text details with content specific to your project.

3: Replace the images in the template by uploading and dragging your desired images into place on the template.

4: Once satisfied with your customizations, click the download button to save your design to your device. Choose the appropriate file format (PNG, JPG, or PDF) and resolution for your intended use.

- You'll find the Layout Links after the Bonus Chapter.

Easy peasy! Get started today and let your creativity soar!

Share (Collaborative)

Now hiring

Intro - Photographer

Participatory Proof

Airline Offering

Intro - PR

Book Launch

Travel Fam Tour

Intro - CEO

Splash It!

Elevate Your Brand

Whether you're an aspiring influencer, startup founder, or seasoned professional, mastering the art of Media Whispering can open doors to endless possibilities. Like any relationship worth cultivating, consistent communication – quality over quantity, is key. Consistently deliver on your promises or commitments.

Introducing yourself to bloggers and media representatives in the ever-evolving digital media landscape has never been easier. Craft your narrative, engage thoughtfully, launch with enticing propositions, and let your mission, values, and achievements shine. Apply the Splash It principles to present irresistible proposals.

Share your story. Highlight your unique background, expertise, and passion. Craft a concise, engaging narrative showcasing your experiences and love for your field to establish authority.

Proof through participation. Show genuine interest in an influencer or media representative's work by engaging with their content on social media. Leave thoughtful comments that demonstrate your knowledge of their niche. Dialoging and asking insightful questions is a great way to introduce yourself to an influencer or journalist.

Launch with an enticing proposition: Present a compelling idea or collaboration opportunity that aligns with their interests and audience. Offer something valuable – an innovative product or skills.

Articulate your mission, values, achievements, and unique selling points. Highlight noteworthy milestones, accolades, or successful collaborations that establish your credibility and expertise in your field. Keep it brief and compelling.

Showcase your expertise, unique insights, opinions, or solutions to challenges to showcase your experience and background. Share specific examples or success stories that demonstrate your value. Provide links to samples of your work, case studies, or testimonials.

Headlines that grab attention and pique curiosity will help you host collaborative proposals, guest posts, or interviews for maximum enticement.

Introduce yourself. A well-crafted introduction can pave the way for fruitful collaborations, influential partnerships, and a thriving media presence. Show how your brand offerings align with their audience's needs or aspirations. Provide contact detail and links to your website or more information. Turn to the Introduce chapter.

Troubleshoot challenges: Identify their audience's pain points and propose how your expertise or offerings can effectively address them. Position yourself as a valuable resource.

Ready to take the plunge? Then, let's jump in.

SHARE

A CURATED COLLECTION

WHETHER YOU'RE UNVEILING A new venue, sharing industry insights, or showcasing technological advancements, the power of a well-crafted press release can inspire your audience to spread the news. Tell your story by putting yourself in the shoes of what a publicist might say.

Here's an example.

"At Flaming Lorraine, we understand the importance of conveying your news and announcements.

"We're passionate about helping you tell your story in a way that captivates media interest.

"Our team creates press releases that forge connections, showcase your brand, and resonate with your target audience.

"From captivating collaborations to fine county roadhouse round-ups, we're proud to share stories that resonate with your target audience.

"Flaming Lorraine can create a press release that captures attention, drives engagement, and amplifies your message. Let's work together."

Share A Collaboration

Sample press release for a music/fashion collaboration.

FOR IMMEDIATE RELEASE

A Harmonious Symphony of Style and Sound

Miramba and Dresswell Collaboration Transforms Music and Fashion Industry

[City, Date] - In a trailblazing collaboration poised to transform the fashion and music world, melody maestro Murray Miramba and couture diva Diana Dresswell have united their extraordinary talents to create an unprecedented fusion of sound and style.

As Miramba and Dresswell embark on a transformative journey transcending traditional artistic boundaries, prepare to be captivated by an unparalleled sensory experience. The highly anticipated showcase of their collective genius promises to push the boundaries of creativity, blurring the lines between art forms and embracing the infinite possibilities that emerge when visionary minds converge.

- **For interview requests** or additional information, contact: [Flaming Lorraine] [flaminglorraine@email.com] [0123 45678]

- **Further Details:** For more information about this groundbreaking collaboration and to stay updated on the latest developments, visit [Website URL]. High-resolution images, artist bios, and additional press materials are available for download on the website's media page.

- Follow Marimba and Dresswell on social media for behind-the-scenes glimpses, exclusive content, and exciting updates:

- [Mariba] Instagram: [Instagram Handle]

- [Dresswell] Instagram: [Instagram Handle]

- **Note to Editors:** High-resolution images, exclusive interviews, and additional media assets are available upon request. Please get in touch with Flaming Lorraine to access these resources or arrange interviews with Marimba and Dresswell.

Share a Gaming Experience

Sample press release for the launch of a new game.

Embark on the Ultimate Virtual Odyssey with GameQuest

[City, Date] – Brace yourself for an unparalleled gaming experience as GameQuest, the highly anticipated game, invites you on an exhilarating virtual journey. Cutting-edge graphics, immersive storytelling, and an all-star cast of characters set a new standard in the gaming industry. Redefine the genre with its breathtaking visual effects.

Say goodbye to information overload and hello to streamlined efficiency. Experience the seamless integration of technology and simplicity as GameQuest empowers you to take control of your digital life.

Get ready to embark on the ultimate virtual odyssey as "GameQuest" gears up for its imminent release, promising to redefine the way you game.

Contact: [Flaming Lorraine] [Media Contact Email] [Media Contact Phone]

Share a Roadhouse Trail

Here's a feature idea for people on the move. Customize or mix up the paragraphs. Make comparisons.

FOR IMMEDIATE RELEASE

Hit the Road(house), Jack!

The Cadillac Association and Cali Tourism round up retro 50s American Diner Vibe county roadhouses

Intro – Some attach grid trays to their car windows, while others embrace the open-road spirit with mouthwatering burgers, hot dogs, and double-thick milkshakes. Think two-tone floor tiles, American diner-style fittings, and pulsing neon signs. It's time to rev up your engines and embark on a delicious road trip to explore (county)

- Situated at (Address), (Venue Name) has become a beloved **parking lot hangout** in (City). Lightning-fast service and unbeatable value-for-money fast food make this place a must-visit. Immerse yourself in the nostalgic 50s ambiance as servers, dressed in (iconic attire), take your order and swiftly deliver it to your window.

- Step into **a bygone era** at (Venue Name), where red vinyl seating and checkerboard floors (set the stage for an authentic American diner experience. While feasting on mouthwatering (Name a Menu Item) and delectable (Name Another Menu Item), enjoy the captivating performances of an Elvis impersonator crooning about his blue suede shoes. It's a scene straight out of the 50s! Go, cat, go!

- Located just (42 km) north of (City) on the picturesque stretch of the (Sunshine) Coast, (Venue Name) has been **a beloved destination** since (Date/Time Reference).

- This **beachside oasis** hasn't lost any of its 70s surfer charms and continues to enchant visitors with its laid-back atmosphere. Forget cholesterol concerns and indulge in delicious, calorie-laden treats. Don't miss the iconic 'Tsunami Burgers' - a specialized menu offering that perfectly complements their gourmet milkshakes. Enjoy breathtaking views of (Name of a Beach) or soak up that everlasting summer feeling.

- Under the ownership of (Owner Name), (Venue Name) has grown from a small establishment with (Number) employees to a thriving destination with (a significantly larger) team. This roadhouse, located at (Address), is renowned for its (legendary pizzas) that barely fit through the car window. Delight in favorites like (Name Some Menu Items) or tasty salads. This **iconic roadhouse** lights up like Bright Week celebrations in Greece. You can't miss it.

- But (Your City) has more to offer hungry motorists! Make your way to (Venue Name) at (Address), where street-food classics receive a delightful **Mexican twist.** Open daily from (Service Hours); this tantalizing spot promises an array of sinful temptations. While they may not align with your beach body goals, who can resist the mouthwatering chicken wraps (or alternative specialty)? It's an experience to savor!

For more information, please visit (Website or contact details).

Customize Exercise

Showcasing a restaurant

Pointers:

1. **Define the unique vibe:** Identify and summarize your venue's distinctive atmosphere or theme. Is it a retro American diner or a laid-back beachside oasis?

2. **Highlight standout features:** Is it lightning-fast service, unbeatable value-for-money, captivating performances, or breathtaking views?

3. **Set the scene:** Immerse your readers in your venue's ambiance and detailed setting. Is it reminiscent of a bygone era or ultra-modern?

4. **Convey temptation:** Capture the deliciousness of your signature dishes - iconic burgers, gourmet pizzas, or unique twists on street-food classics.

5. **Share success stories:** Mention key milestones, ownership changes, or notable expansions in a sentence that reflects your venue's growth and achievements.

Apply similar pointers to any of the above templates.

- **Customize the collaborative press release template.** https://rb.gy/inn2v

Scan me with your phone.

YOUR NAME OR BRAND  Your Website URL goes here

PRESS RELEASE

FOR IMMEDIATE RELEASE

Month, Day, Year

A HARMONIOUS SYMPHONY OF A HEADLINE GOES HERE

Collaboration Transforms [Name Your Industry] As Award-Winning Musician and Renowned Fashion Designer Join Forces to Redefine The [Name Your Industry] landscape - write your blurb or intro here.

City, Date] - In a trailblazing collaboration poised to transform the fashion and music world, critically acclaimed musician [Artist Name], and the award-winning fashion designer [Name], have united their extraordinary talents to create an unprecedented fusion of sound and style.

As [Artist Name] and [Designer Name] embark on a transformative journey transcending traditional artistic boundaries, prepare to be captivated by an unparalleled sensory experience.

The highly anticipated showcase of their collective genius promises to push the boundaries of creativity, blurring the lines between art forms and embracing the infinite possibilities that emerge when visionary minds converge.

Further Details: For more information about this groundbreaking collaboration and to stay updated on the latest developments, visit [Website URL]. High-resolution images, artist bios, and additional press materials are available for download on the website's media page.

Note to Editors: High-resolution images, interviews, and additional media assets are available on request. Please contact [Media Contact Name] to access these resources or to arrange interviews with [Artist Name] and [Designer Name].

Yours Sincerely,

Your Name
CEO

 Your email here

 Your phone number goes here

 Your Website URL goes here

 Your facebook page goes here   Your instagram goes here   Your Youtube channe;;here

PROOF

PARTICIPATION AND COMMITMENT

Consumer cynicism is at an all-time high today, where controversial issues can quickly polarize opinions. Like most things, jumping on the controversy bandwagon can either go brilliantly or fail catastrophically. Choose your collaborators and target influencers wisely.

Virtue signaling or touting convenience, competence, and superiority over competitors alone won't cut it. Bridge the trust gap and back it up. Show authenticity and integrity. Mind how you go, and let your actions speak louder than words.

10 Proof Sprinkles

1. **Corroboration** is your main spice. Back it up with independent sources, glowing testimonials, or rave reviews. Quote industry influencers and share real-life stories on your website, social media platforms, or marketing materials highlighting the benefits your readers or audience reaped.

2. Unveil the creative or **mechanical process** that brings your product or service to life. Take people behind the scenes.

3. Sprinkle in **data and statistics** to support your impressive effectiveness or impact claims. Statistica.com and https://www.google.com/publicdata/directory offer a wide range of research data.

4. Leverage the **power of validation**. Encourage satisfied customers to share their experiences using branded hashtags or tagging your account. Repost and share this user-generated social proof to amplify positive sentiments and showcase real-life interactions with your book or brand.

5. Create success stories with **detailed case studies** showing how your services solved problems or delivered exceptional results.

6. **Monitor and respond** to reviews and ratings on social media platforms and review websites. Positive reviews serve as powerful social proof, while addressing negative feedback demonstrates your commitment to customer satisfaction.

7. If your work has been recognized with **certifications and accreditations**, flaunt them!

8. Allow potential customers **interactive experiences** with trials or free samples.

9. Share **valuable insights and educational content** to establish yourself as a thought leader or go-to authority.

10. Get **celebrity endorsements**. A celebrity is anyone in your field with more followers than you.

Proof of Participation

Introducing Sir Moola McRichpants, a visionary champion of perception management and advocate for active engagement. With a profound belief in the transformative power of participation, Sir Moola loves stirring controversy to highlight the challenges marginalized communities face.

CEO Trades Suit for Tutu

Subhead: Sir Moola McRichpants twirls in the face of convention for a worthy cause.

Blurb: Marvel as this industry titan swaps his boardroom swagger for a pair of delicate ballet pumps, all in the name of charity and sheer hilarity!

New York, NY - In an astonishing turn of events, the illustrious CEO of PrestigeCorp, Sir Moola McRichpants, will put his business acumen to the test on the grandest of stages – a ballet performance! At 6 pm on June 15, at the magnificent Gotham Theater, Sir Moola will twirl, leap, and pirouette alongside other tech execs, executing synchronized grand jetés and pas de deux in an Amorous Swan performance.

Last month, he and his male colleagues donned red strappy stilettos and paraded down the aisles of their stores to raise awareness for widows and orphans in need.

"I love nothing more than bringing a smile to children's faces. If that means donning a tutu, then my colleagues and I are too, too happy to do it for them," joked Sir Moola.

Tickets are available on the event website. Half the proceeds go directly to the We Care Widows & Orphans Foundation. Prepare to be dazzled and thoroughly entertained in this evening of high camp, balletic brilliance, and unbridled amusement.

Join us on this unforgettable journey as Mr. Moneybags leaves his mark on the stage and in the hearts of those in need.

For media inquiries, contact: Amanda Sparkle, Public Relations Manager PrestigeCorp Phone: (555) 123-4567. Email: amanda:sparkle@prestigecorp.com

- **Customize the Participation Layout template**
  https://tinyurl.com/4zr878vz

Scan me with your phone.

Template Images: Generated by AI

Prove Your Philanthropy

FOR IMMEDIATE RELEASE

[Name] Spearheads Philanthropic Initiative to Finance Ambitious Nature Conservation Project

[CITY, DATE] - [Your Organization Name], in collaboration with esteemed leaders from governmental, business, and philanthropic sectors, is leading a cross-sector effort to increase funding for nature conservation. This groundbreaking initiative aims to secure innovative proposals to finance nature's protection, restoration, and preservation in recognition of the undeniable link between a healthy environment and a resilient global economy.

Halting the unchecked destruction of nature is crucial, not only for humanity's well-being but also for our planet's sustainability. To address this critical issue, influential leaders in business and philanthropy will gather to present their pledges to support a 10-year strategy to halt biodiversity loss.

Developing nations, entrusted with safeguarding most of the world's biodiversity, face pressing challenges in balancing conservation efforts with their ongoing human development. Therefore, this initiative will emphasize providing increased financial assistance and incentives to ensure the preservation of natural areas alongside sustainable progress.

The Nature Finance Forum from [Dates] is the first of a series of events dedicated to the Nature Finance and Biological Diversity initiative.

Leading corporation [Company Name] has joined the NFBD initiative by pledging [An amount or promise] to inspire other businesses and communities to participate in helping protect our invaluable natural heritage.

Distinguished participants and panelists at the Nature Finance Forum include:

[Names from the various sectors]

Self-Made Philanthropist's Journey Inspires Millions

[City, Date] - Brace yourself for an awe-inspiring story of resilience, determination, and generosity as self-made philanthropist [Name] shares their remarkable journey. Overcoming adversity and building an empire from scratch, [Name] has touched countless lives and positively impacted society.

His story is a testament to the power of perseverance and compassion.

Contact: [Media Contact Name] [Media Contact Email] [Media Contact Phone]

Customize Exercise

Pointers:

1. **Define the event:** Craft a captivating headline and subhead to pique interest.

2. **Highlight the purpose:** Is it charity, nature conservation, or inspiring others through resilience and generosity?

3. **Set the stage:** Describe what attendees can expect to experience.

4. **Emphasize the impact:** Showcase positive outcomes the event or initiative expects to achieve.

5. **Highlight notable participants:** Mention or quote any influential leaders or individuals involved in the event or initiative.

www.yourwebsite.com

CEO TRADES HIS SUIT FOR TUTU

Sir Moola McRichpants twirls in the face of convention

Marvel as this industry titan swaps his boardroom swagger for a pair of delicate ballet pumps, all in the name of charity and sheer hilarity!

MORE INFORMATION

Amanda Sparkle, PRO Prestige Corp
Phone: (555) 123-4567
Email:
amanda.spark@prestigecorp.com

New York, NY — In an astonishing turn of events, the illustrious CEO of PrestigeCorp, Sir Moola McRichpants, will put his business acumen to the test on the grandest of stages – a ballet performance! At 6 pm on June 15, at the magnificent Gotham Theater,

Sir Moola will twirl, leap, and pirouette alongside other tech execs executing synchronized grand jetés and pas de deux in an Amorous Swan performance.

Last month he and his male colleagues donned red strappy stilettos and paraded down the aisles of their stores to raise awareness for widows and orphans in need. "I love nothing more than bringing a smile to children's faces. If that means donning a tutu, then my colleagues and I are too, too happy to do it for them," joked Sir Moola.

Tickets are available on the event website. Half the proceeds go directly to the We Care Widows & Orphans Foundation. Prepare to be dazzled and entertained in this evening of high camp, balletic brilliance, and unbridled amusement.
Join us on this unforgettable journey as Mr. Moneybags leaves his mark on the stage and in the hearts of those in need.

For media inquiries, contact: Amanda Sparkle, Public Relations Manager PrestigeCorp Phone: (555) 123-4567 Email: amanda.sparkle@prestigecorp.com

LAUNCH

LEAVE A LASTING IMPRESSION

No matter what you're launching, inspire action by emphasizing benefits. You must understand your audience's preferences and pain points to do so. The same applies if you're reaching out to individuals or businesses to explore mutually beneficial opportunities for cross-promotion.

When contacting influencers, journalists, or key stakeholders, always extend a complimentary personalized invitation to experience your product. Tickets to any event should always be for a minimum of two.

If you're launching a book, offer a secret link to access exclusive content or a preview. For example, read the preface, introduction, and first chapter of *Write 6 Successful Self-Publishing Strategies on a Shoestring*.

Cultivate a sense of community by engaging with your audience. Respond to their feedback, and create a space for them to connect around your offering.

Use social media platforms and email newsletters to share intriguing behind-the-scenes tidbits to create buzz and build anticipation.

Conclude with a memorable call-to-action, inviting them to take the next step in any collaboration.

Express your enthusiasm and genuine desire to work together. It's what I call the *hyggelig* approach.

How To Launch a Book

Summarize your book in six soundbites or short sentences.

Here's an example using *Write, 6 Successful Self-Publishing Strategies on a Shoestring*

1. **Filled with** insider secrets and strategies, *Write* offers practical solutions to navigate the publishing journey without unraveling your money sock.

2. **The author offers a fresh perspective by** integrating Fire, Water, Air, Earth, Metal, and Hygge elements into the writing and publishing process.

3. A glossary with more than **101 free resources** empowers you to explore your authorpreneurial realm.

4. *Write* offers **step-by-step guidance** on the most important aspects of self-publishing, including **cover design, DIY editing,** efficient navigation of the social media landscape, and **time-saving Chatbot prompts.**

5. **Practical tips, techniques, and insider secrets** tailored to cash-strapped indie authors make *Write* **an indispensable companion** for anyone seeking self-publishing success.

6. *Write* empowers you to turn your half-finished manuscripts into masterpieces without breaking the bank.

By providing insights on designing covers, establishing a solid work foundation, sparking inspiration, igniting imaginations, and generating reviews, *Write 6 Successful Self-Publishing Strategies on a Shoestring* equips you with the necessary knowledge and tools to ignite your projects.

Write A Press Release

This release is for the book you have in your hands.

Customization Meets Marketing Magic!

Blurb: Launched today, *Splash It!* is your DIY guide to promoting like a pro without the pricey publicist!

Attention is scarce. Competition is fierce. Budget restraints preclude hiring a publicist. You have to market your product or venue yourself, but where to start? Look no further. This press release prompt guide has everything you need to succeed.

Splash It! 99 Customizable Press Release Tools, Texts & Layout Templates will spark your creativity with media-friendly texts, adaptable A4 layout templates to maintain brand personality, and crafty Media Whispering hacks.

Aimed at beginners, ***Splash It!*** takes the time-consuming guesswork out of compiling a press release, drafting an introductory proposal, showcasing an offering, or troubleshooting.

Authored by an award-winning journalist, ***Splash It!*** helps you Share, Participate, Launch, Announce, Showcase, Host, Introduce, and Troubleshoot. Customized exercises guide the novice through each step.

A bonus chapter from *Write – 6 Successful Self-publishing Strategies on a Shoestring* (Hygge Books) exposes common misconceptions, urging against spamming journalists with 'one-size-fits-all announcements.

Says Caroline Hurry, "The need for DIY marketing for freelancers and home business owners uncovered a niche for 'paint-by-paragraphs type' prompts, customizable layout templates, and troubleshooting strategies. ***Splash It!*** is a starting point for anyone needing to promote an upcoming book, product, skill, announcement, familiarization tour, or venue."

Level up your marketing game with free tools and insider tips. Drench the world in your genius. Dip in anywhere, jumpstart your creativity, and make waves with ***Splash It!***

Splash It! 99 Customizable Press Release Tools, Texts & Layout Templates

Publisher: Hygge Books

Author: Caroline Hurry

Publication Date: Fill it in.

Availability: Amazon and other leading bookstores.

Note to editors: Review copies available on email request.

- Download your customizable book launch template here : https://tinyurl.com/ydjdw5w7

Scan me with your phone.

Spark Feature Ideas Around Your Book

Linking your book with a date such as Halloween for a horror tale, for example, increases your chances of publicity. Give magazines a three-month lead. If approaching a weekly newspaper, two to three weeks should be sufficient.

The following 'feature-type' release for Flow 21 Secrets To Refresh Your Relationship. *earned me generous space in* Independent Newspapers *and* Get It! *magazines due to the timing (Valentine's Day).*

Date: Embargoed until late January/early February

Seize the romantic reins and rule this Valentine's

Do you feel more true blue than red hot on Valentine's Day? You're not alone. Wait. You *are* alone. That's the blues thing. Unless you have a few half-sized bottles of sparkling wine – and we know how long those last – where's the fun in popping the cork for one?

Your red heart rages because there hasn't been a word from Conman Don since you wired him the money he needed for his knee operation while stranded in Bali. Not even a thank you. Worse, you can no longer see his profile picture or status on WattsApp.

You thought you'd be feasting on prawns and sunning yourself on the beach with him by now. But you're not. You're eating tuna from the tin, picking at your cuticles, and wondering why empaths are catnip to losers.

Saint Valentine was beheaded at the behest of Emporer Claudius The Cruel for conducting marriages against his wishes. Seems unfair. All love, light, and kiss the bride one minute, locked in jail, penning a heartfelt letter to his jailer's daughter the next. At least, with Claudius The Cruel, you knew where you were. The name alone was a clue.

These days, the likes of Narcissist Nick, Gaslighter Gary, and Stingy Steve come clothed as Cupid, dazzling you with derring-do tales. They pierce your heart with poisoned arrows. They trade in Tinder and tall tales that enable commercial romance pedlars to triple their prices on February 14.

When you come off Cloud Nine, and reality hits, you're in a cold, dark pool of self-pity, berating yourself for letting Boomerang Bruce and Hardluck Harry drain your energy, goodwill, and finances. When did you become a sitting duck for psycho-poachers? Where did you miss the signs? How did you allow some goalpost-shifting, pompous mansplainer to order for you in a restaurant without asking about your preferences or allergies?

When he wasn't thumping his tub about the extraterrestrial origins of viruses or apocalypsing over random conspiracy theories, he piled your misdemeanors – your "booze-induced belligerence, your rudeness to his mother" like coins to feed a slot machine, hitting a triple 7 in the victim row every time. Wait. When did you disrespect his mother?

Oh, you know, the time she arrived unannounced and moved in for three months. She said she felt unwelcome. She doesn't like you.

Looking back with an appraising eye, did you turn a 'love-is-blind' eye to any of these seven red flags?

1. Online, he addresses you as 'Respected Dear,' 'Beautiful Lady,' or gets too familiar too soon

2. Asks to borrow money for any reason

3. Does not return calls and texts timeously

4. Delays and evades – you've never met his friends or family

5 He sulks, withdraws, and stonewalls you

6. You find yourself walking on eggshells around him

7. He's negative, stingy, a resentful tipper, and constantly complains.

Flow 21 Secrets to Refresh Your Relationships (Hygge Books) will teach you how to repel a rogue by trusting red flags and patterns over potential or apologies. If you've slipped on the treacherous rocks of romance or fallen in love with 'potential' for too long, it's an outstretched hand. Says the author: "When you raise the bar by realizing you have everything you need to create everything you want, few will get to undermine you."

- Discover more dating secrets. Look inside here.

- Book: Flow 21 Dating Secrets to Refresh Your Relationships

- Publisher: Hygge Books (LLC)

- Available from Amazon https://amzn.to/3X3k4Tw

SCAN ME

Customize Exercise 1

Pointers

1. **Identify the core message**: What central idea do you want to impart? Summarize it in a concise sentence.

2. **Highlight unique elements:** Craft a sentence highlighting a fresh approach, individual perspective, or whatever sets your book apart from others in your genre.

3. **Explore targeted benefits:** Encapsulate in a sentence how your work can help or inspire readers.

4. **Showcase practical guidance:** Summarize actionable steps readers can take to impart practical value.

5. **Incorporate personalization:** Integrate specific elements that resonate with your personal experiences, anecdotes, or expertise.

6. **Communicate desired outcomes:** Define in a sentence the effects or results readers can expect after engaging with your book.

Customize Exercise 2

Pointers:

1. Ensure your headline syncs with your book title.

2. Explore themes.

3. Highlight key features. A romp through chapters can provide a glimpse into the book's contents.

4. Showcase expertise: [Author Name] has helped countless individuals make genuine connections.

5. Include a call to action and book details: Take charge of your love life today! Grab your copy now.
[Provide a link to PDF for a review copy] Available [Provide a Link].

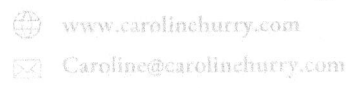

BOOK RELEASE

Trailblaze on a Budget!

If you've been held back by the potential costs of self-publishing or watched your book collect dust on the bottom shelf, *Write 6 Successful Self-Publishing Strategies on a Shoestring* is your game-changer.

- Filled with insider secrets, strategies, and practical solutions to navigate the publishing journey without breaking the bank.
- A glossary with 101 free resources empowers you to explore your entrepreneurial realm, from the cover design to DIY editing on a shoestring.
- Step-by-step guidance on self-publishing's most important aspects, from efficient navigation of the social media landscape to secret time-saving Chatbot prompts.
- DIY techniques for writing, editing, formatting, and launching your book with minimal outlay.
- Tap into the hidden powers of Fire, Water, Air, Earth, Metal, and Hygge to transform your writing journey.
- Learn how to establish a solid foundation and reach, turn inspiration into actionable results, captivate readers with compelling copy, generate reviews, and easily navigate social media.
- A treasure trove of free tools lets your creativity soar as you unleash your unique Fire, Water, Air, Earth, Metal, and Hygge elements into self-discovery, creativity, and transformational growth.
- The author offers a fresh perspective on a practical transformative journey by integrating Nature's elements into the writing and publishing process.

A cracking read!

David White, *The Authority Figure*

Author Image Goes Here

Write 6 Successful Self-Publishing Strategies on a Shoestring is available from Amazon and leading bookstores
bit.ly/42lQfzt

Release Date: [Fill in your release date]
Price: [$9 or fill in your price]

For a PDF or early Kindle copy for review, please email [caroline@carolinehurry.com] with a link to any previous reviews.

ANNOUNCE

Start Spreading the News

The art of announcing holds immense power. Whether introducing a sponsored wine event, unveiling a scientific breakthrough, forging an unstoppable alliance, celebrating an anniversary, or promoting new job opportunities, these templates have you covered.

Announce a Sponsored Wine Event

FOR IMMEDIATE RELEASE

Journey Through The Fruit Flavors at the 25th Olivia Oakbarrel Bacchanalian Banqueters Bash

[City], Date — Olivia Oakbarrel will unveil her latest innovation – wine wheels tailored to individual palates – at the 25th Bacchanalian Banqueters Bash on (Date) at the prestigious (venue name).

Designed to help wine enthusiasts define and refine their selection by sampling offerings from various regions, every Banqueters Bash attendee will receive one to help them curate their tasting list at the annual celebration of [your country]'s top winemakers and merchants.

Indulge in bespoke wines showcased at (your City's) most anticipated annual event. Oenophile activities include:

• **Sabrage skills:** Learn to slice the cork off a bottle of champagne with a saber.

• **Tour de** (your region): The esteemed Amelia Vine of the Riesling Renegades leads attendees on a delightful journey through the finest (your country) wines.

• **Salt and Wine Tasting:** Explore the fascinating interplay between salty foods and wines. Discover how flavors evolve and transform.

• **Exclusive Cellar-Master Tastings:** Gain unparalleled access to prestigious new talent.

Throughout her 25-year reign in the vineyard domain, Ms. Olivia Oakbarrel remains steadfast in her unwavering pursuit of vintage excellence and commitment to showcasing only the finest wines. Commenting on the upcoming festival, the First Lady of Libations says:

"We are grateful for the Bacchanalian Banqueters' unwavering support over the past two decades. Their continued sponsorship enables us to promote the best each region has to offer."

Unforgettable moments and extraordinary wines are yours for the tasting at the Bash, where Olivia Oakbarrel and her dedicated team await your presence. Embark on a vintage adventure.

- Banqueters Bash tickets cost ($) per person. Buy them at the door or online (supply URL).

- For media inquiries and complimentary tickets to the Bash, please contact:

[Contact Name] [Contact Email] [Contact Phone]

A Toast to Olivia Oakbarrel: Famous for her 25-year dedication to the wine industry, high priestess of the harvest, Olivia Oakbarrel brings together wine enthusiasts, industry leaders, and exceptional wines, creating a platform for exploration, education, and appreciation through her annual Bacchanalian Banqueters Bash.

Announce an In-Studio Concert

The Show Must Go Online

Blurb: Immerse Yourself in the soulful magic of Jazz Jubilee's Unplugged & Soulful Virtual Concert.

[City, Date] - Music enthusiasts and jazz lovers are in for a treat as the soul-stirring Jazz Jubilee takes center stage with an exclusive in-studio concert that promises to transport music aficionados to the heart of New Orleans from August 8 to August 22.

Renowned artists Kiki Beauregard, Thabo LaFontaine, with René Fontenot on guitar and Etienne Broussard on keys, lend their mesmerizing harmonies to the groove tunes that define the soulful essence of jazz. Witness the musical magic unfold!

Indulge in the mesmerizing sounds of Afro-Jazz with the incredible Jazz Jubilee featuring timeless classics like *Whispers of the Bayou, Dance of the Crescent Moon, Melodies from the French Quarter,* and a soul-stirring rendition of *The River's Embrace.* Jazz Jubilee fans can enjoy this stripped-down performance from the comfort of their homes.

- Tickets cost $20. Book through TicketPro and JazzTix to experience New Orleans's soul-soothing sounds from your living room.

- Mark your calendars for the CCMA concert, broadcasting on NOLA TV and streaming from BayouBeats.com on (dates).

- Reserve your virtual seat now at www.jazzjubilee.com and let the music sweep you through the heart of jazz.

- Don't miss this unforgettable experience with the King of Jazz himself - Jazz Jubilee. Unplugged & Soulful will be a week to remember! Join the conversation and share your excitement using #JazzJubilee #UnpluggedAndSoulful #VirtualConcert #NOLA-JazzMagic

- **Note:** Jazz Jubilee's latest critically acclaimed album, Soulful Jamboree (2023), is nominated for a prestigious Crescent City Music Award (CCMA) in the Jazz Fusion category.

- For media inquiries and interview requests, please contact: [Name] [Email Address] [Phone Number]

Announce A Juice Line

Fizzarific Delights - A Burst of Joy in Every Sip!

[Your Store Name], a trailblazer in innovative consumer experiences, proudly unveils its latest creation: the highly anticipated "Fizzarific Delights" product line, bringing an explosion of flavor and delight to the market.

The show's star is "Bubbly Blasters," a playful twist on traditional beverages. An effervescent explosion of tantalizing tastes and flavors like "Tropical Tango," "Berry Blast," and "Citrus Symphony," Bubbly Blasters will transport your taste buds.

Said [Your Name], the visionary mind behind this extraordinary creation. "We believe life should be filled with whimsy and laughter. Fizzarific Delights embodies that philosophy."

Indulge in the magic as Fizzarific Delights hits the shelves of [Your Store Name] locations nationwide on [Launch Date]. Come and experience the burst of joy that only Fizzarific Delights can deliver.

For media inquiries, samples, or further information, contact [Your Contact Information]

About [Your Store Name]:
[Your Name] is dedicated to curating unique and extraordinary consumer experiences. With a passion for pushing boundaries, [Your Name] strives to bring the world joy, wonder, and excitement through our product offerings. Discover more at [Your Website].

Announce a Scientific Breakthrough

FOR IMMEDIATE RELEASE

Introducing Excelsior Labs: Pioneering Breakthroughs That Redefine Possibilities

[City, Date] — Excelsior Labs, a trailblazer in scientific exploration, proudly unveils its latest triumph. Leveraging cutting-edge research and relentless dedication, their visionary team has achieved an unprecedented scientific breakthrough. *(Say what it is.)*

Excelsior Labs reaffirms its commitment to delivering solutions. Stay tuned as Excelsior Labs continues to pave the way for a future brimming with possibilities.

- For media inquiries and interview requests, contact: [Name] [Email Address] [Phone Number]

Announce an Alliance

FOR IMMEDIATE RELEASE

Fusion Solutions and StellarTech Forge an Unstoppable Alliance, Revolutionizing the Industry

[City, Date] — Fusion Solutions and StellarTech, giants in their respective domains, are thrilled to announce their transformative merger of expertise and resources, expected to lead the [industry/sector] into an era of unparalleled growth.

This monumental partnership promises to redefine the landscape of [industry/sector] by delivering unrivaled innovation, unmatched quality, and superior customer experiences. Brace yourself for an exhilarating journey as the synergy between these powerhouses takes center stage.

- For media inquiries and interview requests, contact [Name] [Email Address] [Phone Number]

Announce an Anniversary

FOR IMMEDIATE RELEASE

Celebrate a Decade of Excellence with Eminent Enterprises

[City, Date] — Eminent Enterprises, a distinguished leader in the [industry/sector], proudly commemorates its 10th anniversary, a notable milestone symbolizing a decade of achievements.

Having earned an illustrious reputation for its unwavering commitment to a customer-centric approach and dedication to innovation, Eminent Enterprises reaffirms its commitment to empowering customers, fostering growth, and leaving an indelible mark on the industry.

- For media inquiries and interview requests, contact [Name] [Email Address] [Phone Number]

Announce a Partnership

FOR IMMEDIATE RELEASE

Pathfinders Inc. and Catalyst Solutions: Pioneering Collaboration for a Brighter Future

[City, Date] — Pathfinders Inc., a frontrunner in [industry/sector], and Catalyst Solutions, a creative force in [industry/sector], proudly announce a strategic partnership.

By combining their unrivaled expertise and shared commitment to innovation, Pathfinders Inc. and Catalyst Solutions are poised to revolutionize [industry/sector] through collaborative projects, synergistic ideas, and groundbreaking initiatives. As they embark on this transformative journey together, the partnership promises to create new paradigms, unlock untapped potential, and drive progress.

Witness the birth of a visionary alliance that will shape the future of [industry/sector].

- For media inquiries and interview requests, contact [Name] [Email Address] [Phone Number]

Announce Job Opportunities

FOR IMMEDIATE RELEASE

DynamicTech Industries Unveils Exciting Job Opportunities

[City, Date] - DynamicTech Industries, a trailblazer in cutting-edge technology solutions, is thrilled to announce its new hiring round and the availability of several enticing job positions.

With a solid commitment to talent acquisition and fostering professional growth, DynamicTech Industries provides a platform for ambitious professionals to make a meaningful difference and thrive in the ever-evolving world of technological possibilities.

The company seeks exceptional candidates for the following positions:

Software Engineer:

Required skills include proficiency in programming languages such as Java or Python, strong problem-solving abilities, and experience with software development methodologies.

Responsibilities: Develop and maintain high-quality software solutions, collaborate with cross-functional teams, and contribute to the improvement of products.

Data Scientist:

Required skills include expertise in statistical analysis, data mining, machine learning techniques, proficiency in programming languages such as Python, and strong analytical thinking.

Responsibilities: Extract insights from large datasets, design and implement predictive models.

UX/UI Designer:

Required skills include proficiency in design tools such as Sketch or Adobe Creative Suite, a strong understanding of user-centered design principles, and experience creating intuitive and visually appealing interfaces.

Responsibilities: Collaborate with multidisciplinary teams to create exceptional user experiences, conduct user research and testing.

These positions offer an exciting opportunity to work with cutting-edge technologies, collaborate with talented professionals, and contribute to developing innovative solutions that shape the future.

DynamicTech Industries is committed to creating a work environment where all individuals are valued, empowered, and given equal opportunities for growth and success.

To apply for any of these positions or learn more about career opportunities at DynamicTech Industries, please visit our careers page at [Insert Careers Page URL].

For media inquiries or further information, please contact: [Media Contact Name] [Media Contact Email] [Media Contact Phone]

About DynamicTech Industries: A renowned leader in providing cutting-edge technology solutions, DynamicTech Industries offers a wide range of advanced software solutions, data analytics services, and user experience design expertise, driving digital transformation and success for its clients.

- **To download the Job Opportunities template, click here.** https://tinyurl.com/rucbawa8

Scan me with your phone.

Customize Exercise

Pointers:

1. What is your announcement's main objective?

2. How will your introduction create curiosity or leave a strong impression?

3. How will you communicate the unique value your product brings?

4. How will you engage or leverage key influencers or collaborators to involve them in your launch?

5. What call-to-action will you use?

DynamicTech Industries Launches New Era of Opportunity

DynamicTech Industries is committed to creating a work environment where all individuals are valued, empowered, and given equal opportunities for growth and success.

HIRING NOW

Visit our careers page at [your URL]

To apply for any of these positions or learn more about career opportunities at DynamicTech Industries, please visit our careers page at [Insert Careers Page URL].

For media inquiries or further information, please contact:
[Media Contact Name]
[Media Contact Email]
[Media Contact Phone]

Software Engineer

Required Skills: Proficiency in programming languages,, and experience with software development methodology

UI Designer

Proficiency in design tools such as Sketch or Adobe Creative Suite, strong understanding of user-centered design principles

Data Scientist

Expertise in statistical analysis, data mining, and machine learning techniques,

SHOWCASE

AIRLINES AND VACATION VENUES

LEVERAGE EMOTIONAL TRIGGERS TO effectively communicate the value and benefits of whatever you're showcasing, from an airline to a tourism company to your target audience, viable business, finance, and leisure magazine readers.

For frequent fliers – and I speak from experience – these are convenience, comfort, premium amenities, exceptional service, and ease of passage throughout their journey. Business executives also like bargains, so rewards create a sense of well-being.

Other emotional triggers include relaxation, connection, wonder, freedom to travel, breaking constraints, and embracing new adventures.

Showcase Your Ideas

Present your ideas as listicles with a comparative edge or a brief overview of each one for more editorial appeal. A listicle is a media-friendly copy format that provides quick and easily digestible content.

Combining the elements of a list and an article, it typically features a catchy '10-best' title followed by a list of concise, numbered, or bulleted items.

Each topic – from practical tips to humorous advice – presents as a brief paragraph or sentence, making its easy-to-read structure a favored choice for readers and editors alike. Always make a journalist's life as easy as possible.

Showcase an Airline Offering

For Immediate Release

Headline: Class Action
Can Flying Business Class Provide a Viable Return on Investment?

Blurb: A business-class airline seat can cost five times as much as its economy counterpart. *Skyler Jetson, Chief Executive Officer of Jolly Jetways,* answers questions and explains why he thinks it's worth the price difference of around ($S?) is worth every cent.

A good night's sleep in the clouds under a soft duvet will always beat shoe-horning yourself into the middle stand-by economy seat. Jolly Jetways offer flat beds, slippers, seat control panels, adjustable tables, and privacy screens. *House of Jolly* amenity kits containing eye masks, socks, lip balms *(product name)*, moisturizers, and toothbrushes have everything you need for a refreshing overnight flight.

How much is your comfort and time worth?

That depends on how much you earn," says *Skyler Jetson, Chief Executive Officer of Jolly Jetways.* "If it's around, say, *$1 million* or more a year, then the extra money for the business ticket that allows you to work, sleep, avoid jet lag, and arrive fresh to your meeting, might save you 12 precious productive hours. Time is the new money."

The good news, says Jetson, is that "you could write the business class ticket off as a legitimate expense. Also, thanks to our reward systems, the more you fly, the less you spend. Our corporate programs offer up to 10% discounts, fast-track security, reward flights, and car rentals."

How does Jolly Jetways stay ahead of the game?

"Business class typically accounts for the lion's share of an airline's income, so there's ample incentive to entice corporate fliers, and competition between airlines is fierce. Jolly Jetways goes the extra mile by offering business clients complimentary 4-star hotel stays, city tours, and chauffeur services to and from the airport.."

Apart from priority check-in and an extra (30kg) baggage allowance, Jolly Jetways business class ticket holders enjoy exclusive entry to the tranquil lounge enclave with relaxation areas, shower facilities, and gourmet snacks.

Adds Jetson, "These come from the kitchen of (*name of the chef*), who crafted our new summer menu (p*rovide a link if applicable*) with a *Samuel Sommelier*-inspired boutique wine list, including a rare Sauvignon Blanc from Belize, exclusive to our VIP passengers."

Jolly Jetways just spent (*$ million*) renovating their lounge in (*city name*), which now offers *private massage suites, a library, and an indoor golf simulator.*

Note to editors: A Business Class ticket from (*departure to arrival destination*) costs around (name price). Prices fluctuate, so please check (website address) for updates.

- For an exclusive interview with Skyler Jetson, contact Amanda Sparkle (Supply contact details) or visit their website at (supply address)

Optional: If the publication allows attachment, supply no more than three with a note saying: Attached are low-res images of Skyler Jetson, a Business Class Seat, and dishes from the Summer menu. Higher Res images are available (supply link).

- **Download and customize the Airline Feature Template here**: https://tinyurl.com/bdujavrs

Scan Me With Your Phone.

Showcase Tourist Operator Venues

Game Plan: Top 10 Unforgettable Safari Experiences

Blurb: Embark on a thrilling journey into the heart of southern Africa's untamed wilderness, where close encounters with majestic wildlife, awe-inspiring landscapes, and exclusive accommodations await. From breathtaking whale sightings to guided walks and unique cultural experiences, these 10 handpicked venues from (Name Tourist Operator) promise an unforgettable adventure for discerning travelers seeking the ultimate safari experience.

Best Whale and Penguin Sightings
Location: Cape Town, South Africa
Highlights: Table Mountain, Cape Point, Kirstenbosch Gardens, Boulders Beach
Base Camp: (Name Venue Operator)
Description: Immerse yourself in the beauty of the Atlantic and Indian Oceans while exploring Cape Town's iconic landmarks. Witness endangered African penguins at Boulders Beach and marvel at Southern Right whales along the picturesque whale coast.

Best Fynbos Foot Safari
Location: Garden Route, South Africa
Venue: (Name Your Venue and Safari Operator)
Highlights: Guided walking safaris, biodiversity, Big Five, tented camps
Description: Discover the enchanting Garden Route on foot as expert trail guides lead you through the fynbos-covered landscape. Encounter diverse ecosystems, the Big Five, and an array of antelope species while spending nights in exclusive tented camps.

Best Prehistoric Reserve
Location: Karoo, South Africa
Venue: (Name Your Venue)
Highlights: Fossilized dinosaur footprints, wildlife tracking, ancient rock paintings
Description: Uncover the mysteries of Earth's ancient history. Explore (Name Your Venue), marvel at 250 million-year-old fossils, track cheetahs, and encounter 225 bird species. Sleep under the stars during a thrilling fly camping experience.

Best for Families and Volunteerism
Location: (Name Operator)
Highlights: Wildlife rehabilitation, Hollywood star-favored, volunteer opportunities
Description: Join (Name Venue) in their remarkable conservation efforts. Witness the healing of injured animals at the Rehabilitation Centre and support the nurturing of orphaned wildebeest, buffalo, and zebra calves. Participate in volunteer programs and gain insights into the importance of wildlife conservation.

Best Leopard Location
Location: Sabi Sands Reserve, South Africa
Venue: (Name Operator)
Highlights: Abundant leopards, pristine natural environment, thrilling wildlife sightings
Description: (Venue) offers an unparalleled opportunity to observe thriving leopard populations in all their captivating beauty amid their natural lush riverine habitat.

Best Guided Safari Walking
Location: Klaserie Reserve, South Africa
Venue: (Name Your Operator)
Highlights: Walking safaris, intimate wildlife encounters, traditional folklore
Description: Knowledgeable rangers guide you through Big Five territory, sharing fascinating insights into traditional folklore. Witness breathtaking vistas of the Drakensberg range.

Best Tree House
Location: (Name Reserve
Venue: (Name Operator)
Highlights: Elevated tree house experience, immersion in nature
Description: Embrace your inner explorer and indulge in the unique "Me Tarzan, You Jane" experience. Stay in the reserve's triple-decker forest ship at (Name Venue). Immerse yourself in the sights and sounds of the savannah from your lofty perch under a celestial canopy.

Best Wild Dog Spotting
Location: Madikwe Reserve, South Africa
Venue: (Name Operator)
Highlights: African wild dogs, family-friendly activities, live webcam
Description: Experience the thrill of observing these endangered African wild dogs gathering at the central watering hole. Engage in family-friendly activities and watch the live webcam for captivating wildlife sightings.

Best Tented Camp for Traditional Dancing
Location: (Name Operator),
Highlights: Guaranteed wildlife sightings, Zulu dancing
Description: Immerse yourself in the wonders of the savannah at (Venue). Indulge in the chic safari ambiance of tents and witness captivating Zulu dance performances.

Best Place to Stalk Game with Bushmen
Location: Central Kalahari Reserve, Botswana
Venue: (Name Venue)
Highlights: Rare black-maned lions, Bushmen encounters, immersive cultural experiences
Description: Venture into the vast Central Kalahari Reserve and discover the land of the rare black-maned lions. Engage with the indigenous Bushmen, learn their ancient traditions, and unlock survival secrets in the desert.

- **For more information,** high-resolution images, or to arrange a press trip to any of these extraordinary venues, please contact: Provide your email, website address, and phone number.
  Note: Customize contact details and other information per your publication's requirements.

Customize Exercise

Pointers

1. Use the listicle Top 10 techniques to engage interest.

2. Create a distinct brand identity to help establish recognition.

3. Choose visuals that align with your piece.

4. Identify the preferences, needs, emotional motivations, and interests of your target audience:

5. Determine what sets your offerings apart from others in the market. Showcase unique benefits.

JOLLY JETWAYS MEDIA

For Immediate Release
Date: January 12, 2024

Class Action

Is Flying Business Class a Viable Return on Investment?

:A business-class airline seat can cost five times as much as its economy counterpart. Skyler Jetson, Chief Executive Officer of Jolly Jetways, answers questions and explains why he thinks it's worth the price difference of around ($S?) is worth every cent.

A good night's sleep in the clouds under a soft duvet will always beat shoe-horning yourself into the middle stand-by economy seat. Jolly Jetways offer flat beds, slippers, seat control panels, adjustable tables, and privacy screens. House of Jolly amenity kits containing eye masks, socks, lip balms (product name), moisturizers, and toothbrushes have everything you need for a refreshing overnight flight.

For an exclusive interview with Skyler Jetson, contact Amanda Sparkle (Supply contact details)

www.jollyjetways.com

HOST

A Familiarization Tour

When hosting an exceptional media event, the key is to combine meticulous planning with boundless creativity. Set the stage for an authentic experience that captivates all the senses. Embrace the art of storytelling with details that weave a tapestry of wonder and foster emotional connections with attendees.

Whether a grand opening or an exciting travel tour, hosting an event presents a beautiful opportunity to captivate audiences and make a lasting impression. Inviting journalists on tours to promote a venue or airline requires charm, sophistication, and a touch of whimsy.

Customize Exercise

Design a Media Experience for Your Event

Pointers

1. **Tailor an engaging and diverse itinerary.** Select captivating activities, offer exclusive access to unique locations or experiences, and create opportunities for media representatives to immerse themselves in the key highlights firsthand. Strive to curate moments to leave a lasting impression on attendees.

2. **Prepare a detailed press kit**. Include background information, facts, comprehensive schedules, biographies of key speakers or participants, and relevant visuals. The more you simplify a journalist's work, the better your chances of comprehensive coverage.

3. **Arrange Media Interactions:** Dedicate specific time slots for media interviews and Q&A sessions with key individuals involved in your tour or event. Schedule appointments and create a comfortable interview environment, ensuring journalists can gather exclusive insights, quotes, and valuable content.

4. **Offer engaging visual opportunities during your tour.** Stage photo opportunities or grant access to unique vantage points. Additionally, provide high-quality images and videos to enable the media to incorporate visually appealing content in their coverage.

5. **Cultivate relationships and follow-up.** Take the time to connect with journalists, understand their interests, and establish rapport. After the tour or event, thank the media for their coverage and offer any additional information or resources they may require. Regularly communicate with them to stay on their radar for future opportunities, fostering lasting relationships.

Hosting a Scandinavian Trip

Adapt the following invitation accordingly.

Your Passport to Nordic Treasures!

Subject: **Invitation to Explore Scandinavia with** [Your Company] and [Name of Airline]

Dear [Travel Journalist's Name],

I hope this letter finds you in good health and high spirits. Wanda Lust, travel publicist for [Company Name) here. I am delighted to extend an exclusive invitation to you on behalf of (Airline Company) and [Tour Company].

All three destination itineraries offer unparalleled Scandinavian experiences, promising to deliver fantastic stories and insights for your prestigious readership.

The Itineraries

1. **Keep it Green for Copenhagen Cool**
   (Provide Dates)
   Explore Copenhagen, where design, sustainability, and cultural marvels converge in an environmentally conscious vibe. This compact city on the sea boasts dazzling architecture, Michelin-starred dining, and a commitment to becoming carbon-neutral by 2025.
   Indulge in luxurious accommodations at the esteemed [Add Venue Name]. Uncover the city's hidden gems, from canal tours and lakeside explorations to visits to iconic landmarks such as Nyhaven, Hans Christian Andersen's house, and the renowned Louisiana Museum of Modern Art.

2. **Wild Nights in the Lapp of Luxury**
   (Provide Dates)
   Embark on a thrilling adventure through Northern Sweden's breathtaking landscapes. Immerse yourself in the rich heritage of the Sámi people, indigenous to the region, and witness the untouched beauty of Europe's last wilderness. From the cultural charm of Stockholm to the majestic wonders of Laponia, a UNESCO World Heritage site, awe-inspiring experiences await you.
   Luxurious accommodations at the distinguished [Add Venue Name] ensure a restful retreat after exploring sites like (Name Examples).

3. **Queen of the Castle Contenders**
   (Provide Dates)
   Discover Denmark's regal wonders as you traverse the enchanting castles and historic sites that dot the landscape. From Frederiksborg Castle in Hillerød to the haunted Dragsholm Castle, each location offers a unique glimpse into Danish history and architecture.
   Relax in luxurious comfort at the esteemed [Add Venue Name] and savor Nordic terroir cuisine prepared by the renowned chef (Add Name). Visits to Egeskov Castle, Kokkedal Slot, and Kronborg ensure an immersive experience showcasing Denmark's traditional grandeur.

[Your Company] proudly announces our partnership with [Airline Name], providing exclusive flights for each tour to and from your respective cities. We cordially invite you to join us on these extraordinary tours, allowing you to delve into each destination's beauty, history, and unique experiences.

Your standing as a respected travel journalist lends immense value to portraying the essence of these remarkable journeys to your readers, and we would be delighted to host you.

To learn more about the itineraries, exclusive accommodations, and exceptional experiences that await you, please refer to the attached detailed itineraries for each tour. We believe these curated journeys will provide a wealth of captivating content for your publication.

We kindly request your response by [RSVP Date] to confirm your interest and availability. Should you have any questions or require further information, please contact me directly at [Your Phone Number] or [Your Email Address].

We would be honored to have you as our guest and look forward to embarking on this remarkable adventure together.

Yours sincerely,

Wanda Lust

- Wanda Lust specializes in devising innovative promotional strategies, bringing events to life, and creating unforgettable moments. Through meticulous planning and a keen eye for detail, Wanda Lust makes memories with every event and familiarization trip she hosts.

- **Customize the Familiarization Tour Template here.** https://tinyurl.com/2p9yfp2n

Scan me with your phone.

Your Name: Or Brand Here
Phone number: 1234567
Email address: yourname@youcompamy.cpm

Your Logo Here

UNVEILING NORDIC TREASURES
With [Airline name]

Keep it Green Copenhagen Cool
Provide Dates)

Explore Copenhagen, where design and sustainability converge in an environmentally conscious vibe. Indulge in accommodations at the esteemed [Add Venue Name].
Uncover the city's hidden gems, from canal tours and lakeside explorations to visits to iconic landmarks such as Nyhaven, Hans Christian Andersen's house, and the Louisiana Museum of Modern Art.

Wild Nights, Lapp of Luxury
Provide Dates)

Embark on a thrilling adventure through Northern Sweden's breathtaking landscapes. Immerse yourself in the rich heritage of the Sámi people and witness the untouched beauty of Europe's last wilderness.
 Luxurious accommodations at the distinguished [Add Venue Name] hotel ensure a restful retreat after exploring sites such as (Name Three Examples).

Queen of the Castle Contenders
Provide Dates)

Discover Denmark's regal wonders as you traverse the enchanting castles and historic sites that dot the landscape. From Frederiksborg Castle in Hillerød to the haunted Dragsholm Castle, each location offers a unique glimpse into Danish history and architecture. Relax in luxurious comfort at the esteemed [Add Venue Name] and savor Nordic terroir cuisine prepared by the renowned chef (Add Name). V

INTRODUCE

SET UP PRODUCTIVE RELATIONSHIPS

A WELL-CRAFTED INTRODUCTION PAVES the way to meaningful coverage and fruitful collaborations. Position yourself or your offering as an exceptional choice in a crowded market.

Introduce Yourself Or Your Brand

Leave a lasting impression that resonates with these four tips.

1. **Emphasize** what you or your product can do for them. Anticipate and answer questions about differentiating your service or expertise from the competition.

2. **Enhance** your credibility with *social proof*. Share compelling data, testimonials, case studies, or endorsements to substantiate your assertions.

3. **Cultivate** friendships: An introduction is just the beginning. Provide value, remain authentic, and be responsive in your interactions. Tailor your approach to their interests. Building trust and rapport will ensure long-term partnerships that yield fruitful results.

4. **Provide** value by offering insights, resources, or collaboration opportunities that align with their interests. Stay authentic in your interactions and nurture relationships built on mutual trust and respect.

An Introductory Proposal Template

Save time and ensure consistency with a well-crafted proposal template that helps structure your introduction and aligns your communication with potential clients or media professionals. Clearly articulate your unique value proposition.

7 Key Components

1. **Introduction:** Introduce yourself and your business, highlighting your strengths and unique benefits. Briefly outline your expertise and why you are the right fit for collaboration.

2. **Project Summary:** Clearly outline the key details and objectives of the project or partnership. Provide a concise overview of the value proposition and how it aligns with the recipient's goals.

3. **Scope of Work:** Be specific and detailed. Outline deliverables, timelines, and any particular requirements to ensure your proposal aligns with the client's expectations and avoids misunderstandings.

4. **Methodology:** Describe your approach, highlighting specific tools, techniques, or strategies you will employ. Showcase your experience and expertise in this section, demonstrating your ability to deliver exceptional results.

5. **Budget:** Provide a transparent and detailed breakdown of your proposed budget. Include relevant fees, expenses, and payment terms. This level of transparency helps establish trust and showcases your professionalism.

6. **Authority:** Showcase your strengths, qualifications, and relevant experience. Highlight past successes or notable achievements that demonstrate your capability and credibility.

7. **Call to Action:** Be clear and provide a specific next step for the recipient. Whether requesting a meeting, providing additional information, or expressing their interest, make it easy for them to respond and continue the conversation.

Here are two text examples from Zoom Zelda and Flaming Lorraine you can customize.

Introduce Yourself as a Photographer

Hi [Client's Name],

Zelda of the Zoom Lens here. As a passionate photojournalist, I had to reach out to you after seeing the incredible work your Company does concerning [mention the specific area/industry]. Our collaboration could be a game-changer in leveraging your brand's visual personality to connect with your target audience via a social media strategy that captures your visual narrative with a #capturethemoment hashtag.

Capture The Moment

- **A visual narrative:** Whether it's behind-the-scenes shots, events, or product launches, I will tell your story through striking images that evoke emotions and connect with your audience.

- **Social media strategy:** My visually captivating content drives organic growth on Instagram and Twitter. I will craft compelling captions, incorporate relevant hashtags, and encourage user-generated content to foster a sense of community.

- **Photojournalistic coverage:** As a seasoned photojournalist, I will be on the ground, capturing the moments that matter.

If you'd like to collaborate in creating a captivating visual journey that elevates your brand, please contact me directly at [Email Address] or [Phone].

Warm regards,

Zelda Zoom [Your Name] [Your Company]

- **Customize the Zoom Zelda layout proposal template.** https://tinyurl.com/y5pzh8ce

Scan me with your phone.

Introduce Yourself as a PR Consultant

Flaming Lorraine

Flaming Lorraine is an electrifying media and public relations force known for igniting philanthropic participation in charitable fundraising initiatives. Armed with an innate ability to captivate audiences and connect with diverse communities, Flaming Lorraine's unwavering dedication to perception management – progress through active engagement – sparks inspiration in the transformative power of participation. Ignite your presence!

- **Customize the Flaming Lorraine layout template**
  https://tinyurl.com/ke5dpnn9

Scan me with your phone.

Introduce a Chef Executive Office

Epic Culinary Upgrade for Epicurean Escapes: Meet the New CEO

[Epicurean Escapes], a leading [industry/sector] company, is thrilled to announce the appointment of Olivia Martinez [Name] as the new chief executive Officer (CEO). With a wealth of culinary expertise and a proven track record of success, [Ms. Martinez] brings a fresh perspective and visionary leadership to our organization.

With a keen understanding of our discerning customers' evolving tastes, [Name] is a respected culinary professional with an extensive background in (name it). She will establish new culinary frontiers, ensuring that [Company] remains at the forefront of innovative gastronomy and customer satisfaction.

[Epicurean Escapes]'s [MD] Ralf Russo said, "[Ms. Martinez)] brings expertise, leadership, and creativity to our organization."

Ms. Martinez said. "I am honored to join the [Company Name] family and passionate about creating exceptional dining experiences."

About: [Epicurean Escapes] is a [description of the Company's core business/industry/sector]. With a reputation for excellence and a commitment to delivering exceptional products/services, [Company] has established itself as a trusted name in the [industry/sector]. Through innovation, quality, and customer-centricity, [Company Name] continues to set new standards and exceed expectations.

For media inquiries, contact Flaming Lorraine at [phone number, email address)

Note to editors: High-resolution images and additional information are available upon request.

- **Customize the CEO template here.**
  https://bit.ly/3NGGiHE

Scan me with your phone.

Introduce A Product Line

FOR IMMEDIATE RELEASE

Introducing the Marveluxe Collection: An Extravaganza of Innovation and Style

[City, Date] - Get ready to experience unparalleled luxury and innovation as [Store Name], the industry's visionary trendsetter, unveils its latest triumph: the Marveluxe Collection. This groundbreaking product line will revolutionize your everyday life.

Imagine stepping into a world where imagination meets reality, ordinary becomes extraordinary, and innovation knows no bounds. The Marveluxe Collection brings you a range of delightfully whimsical and ingeniously practical creations that will elevate your lifestyle with the following products.

- **The Fluxomatic Blender**: Effortlessly transform your everyday ingredients into culinary masterpieces and make magic in your kitchen. With its self-stirring capabilities and intuitive control panel, the Fluxomatic Blender makes cooking fun.

- **The Envirosphere Air Purifier:** Say goodbye to stale air and hello to a breath of fresh innovation with this revolutionary device that harnesses advanced technology to recycle clean, revitalizing air throughout your home.

- **The Nebula Garden:** This unique indoor garden – a mesmerizing fusion of art and greenery – brings the wonders of nature into your living space with its self-sustaining ecosystem and captivating LED light display. Sit back, relax, and enjoy the Nebula enchantment in a world of serenity.

- **The HarmoniMelody Speaker:** Unleash a symphony of sound in a stunningly compact design. Immerse yourself in the rich, crystal-clear audio produced by wireless connectivity. A dynamic range will revolutionize your listening experience.

The Marveluxe Collection is an invitation to indulge in a world of wonder and innovation. With each creation meticulously crafted to spark joy and ignite your imagination, [Store Name] is proud to bring this exceptional collection to life.

Be the first to immerse yourself in the magic of the Marveluxe Collection at our grand unveiling event on [Event Date] at [Event Location]. Join us for an evening of demonstrations, exclusive offers, and prizes.

For more information, contact: [Media Contact Name] [Title] [Email Address] [Phone Number]

About: [Store Name] is a leading innovator in the retail industry, constantly pushing the boundaries of what's possible. With a commitment to delivering exceptional quality and unique experiences, [Store Name] has earned a reputation as a trailblazer in innovative products and services.

Introduce a Safari Lodge

FOR IMMEDIATE RELEASE

Escape to the Untamed Beauty of (Name of Venue): An Unforgettable Safari Adventure Awaits

For an extraordinary weekend getaway combining family-friendly excitement with the thrill of an authentic safari experience, look no further than (Name of Venue), just a two-hour drive from (Name of Airport). With its breathtaking natural surroundings, this hidden gem offers a malaria-free haven for adventurers of all ages.

Nestled amid 600 hectares of indigenous trees, (Name of Venue) boasts 12 distinctive chalets, including a romantic honeymoon suite, providing comfortable and memorable accommodations for solo travelers, couples, and families.

Immerse yourself in the ambiance of African baroque design. Each chalet features an en-suite bath or shower, a well-stocked mini bar fridge, and an espresso machine. Sweeping mountain vistas greet you from your private sun deck, where you can bask in nature's warm embrace.

Situated on the magnificent (Name of Game Farm) game farm on the outskirts of (Name of reserve and region), in (country or province), (Name of Venue) offers unparalleled views of the majestic (Name of Mountain Range). Discover an Afro-chic restaurant, a refreshing pool, and a charming bush bar area that create the perfect romantic ambiance for unwinding.

For corporate retreats or teambuilding getaways, our owner-run lodge can accommodate 24 people) sharing. Gather around a crackling fire, savor traditional meals, forge meaningful connections under the starlit African sky, and make memories.

More than just a safari destination, (Name of Venue) is committed to restoring and rehabilitating the surrounding reserve through innovative game breeding techniques, ensuring the revival of indigenous wildlife species that once roamed this world heritage biosphere. Keep your eyes peeled for playful Vervet monkeys while genets and warthogs add their charm to your African experience.

When you're not relishing the serenity of your surroundings, immerse yourself in the wonders of the wild. Embark on exhilarating game drives, venture into the wilderness on guided walks, hike through picturesque trails, or try fishing. At (Name of Venue), adventure knows no bounds.

Unwind, rejuvenate, and indulge in a traditional bush lodge experience where personalized service and pampering are paramount. Rest easy knowing that your safety is our top priority, with a 24-hour guard patrol ensuring your peace of mind.

- **Special Offer:** As a valued reader of (Publication Name), we invite you to experience the magic of (Name of Venue) with an exclusive discount of 15% on your booking. Mention the promo code "WILDLIFE15" when making your reservation. Terms and conditions apply.

- For more information or to book your extraordinary getaway, (Provide contact details)

Introduce an Innovative Startup

FOR IMMEDIATE RELEASE

Visionary Entrepreneur Revolutionizes Tech Landscape

[City, Date] - Prepare to witness the next giant leap in technological innovation as a creative entrepreneur [Entrepreneur Name] introduces their groundbreaking startup. Armed with cutting-edge solutions and a disruptive mindset, [Entrepreneur Name] has set out to revolutionize how we interact with technology.

Their groundbreaking product promises to transform industries, enhance user experiences, and redefine possibilities. Don't miss the opportunity to be part of this tech revolution.

Contact: (Provide contact details)

#perception management

The Golden Rule

Always thank and acknowledge any complaint

#troubleshooting101

Troubleshoot

Consequences of Customer Offense

Bad press happens. You can embrace it as a chance to showcase your resilience and turn adversity into opportunity. Or you can dig your heels in and make matters worse.

An occasional fall is one thing, but recovery is steeper when trust in your company takes a tumble and share prices plummet.

Publicity blunders pave the road to rock bottom, the hubristic result of ignoring customer expectations.

Stick to selling over-priced merchandise if you're a retail chain and hold the tedious lectures on oxymoronic corporate values, especially when they cancel women's rights.

Recovering from an offensive incident requires introspection, proactive measures, and consistent efforts to align with customer expectations.

Disastrous PR Strategies

The following will lead to a loss of loyalty and reputational damage. Avoid where possible.

1. **Offending Religious Groups:** Avoid implementing policies or actions that offend, divide, or alienate significant portions of the customer base.

2. **Disregarding Customer Values:** Avoid insensitivity to cultural, social, or moral issues. Failure to align with customer values and expectations is a significant misstep.

3. **Protecting one group's preferences at the expense of another's rights:** Avoid any breaches of ethics that sow discord, fuel division, and cast shade over fairness and equality.

4. **Engaging in Bitter Fights and Name-Calling:** Avoid promoting contentious discussions among customers or participating. Doing so fosters a hostile environment, discourages constructive dialogue, erodes trust, and drives customers away.

5. **Ignoring or Blocking Customers:** Avoid sending clear messages of disregard by failing to acknowledge and respond to concerns. Blocking customers on social media will result in a breakdown of trust and customer loyalty.

6. **Believing Any Publicity is Good:** Avoid that old chestnut! Engaging in controversial or offensive actions to gain attention can backfire with long-lasting consequences.

Let's consider two fictional actions that transform public perception by transparently implementing systemic changes and demonstrating a commitment to be better.

A clothing chain faces criticism for allowing men to use their women's fitting rooms to foster inclusivity. The resulting backlash highlights the importance of addressing their female clientele's privacy, respect, sensitivity, and safety concerns.

By providing two additional changerooms – Male and All-Inclusive – the CEO quietens the storm and makes everyone happy.

Facing an outcry when the public learned their supplier violated animal anti-cruelty practices, the CEO terminated the supplier's contract.

She then implemented a robust supplier code of conduct and established partnerships with organizations dedicated to sourcing ethical ingredients for her cosmetics to regain consumer trust.

Crisis Management

Crucial for successful troubleshooting is to adopt a proactive and empathetic approach. Navigate crises and rebuild brand reputation by learning from mistakes, adapting internal processes, engaging stakeholders, and showcasing a genuine commitment to positive change. Here's a 5-point plan.

1. **Acknowledge the concerns** raised by customers and the public. Demonstrate a genuine understanding of the issue's impact and the offense caused.

2. **Offer a sincere apology** to everyone who feels let down by the company's actions. Distance it from offensive ideologies or activities. Clearly, articulate the company's stance and commitment to rectifying the situation.

3. **Take corrective measures**. Publicly terminate any support or partnerships contributing to the offense. Take active steps to align with customer expectations and values by involving them in decision-making.

4. **Engage in open dialogue.** Encourage constructive conversation with customers and stakeholders. Provide platforms and opportunities where they can express their concerns, share feedback, and ask questions. Address their inquiries respectfully and promptly.

5. **Rebuild trust through actions.** Follow through on commitments. Implement initiatives that promote ethical practices, and engage in partnerships that align with the company's values. Transparently communicate these efforts.

3 Ways to Move Forward

1. **Learn and adapt**. Analyze the organizational processes and decision-making frameworks that contributed to the misstep. Implement changes to prevent similar issues from recurring.

2. **Conduct internal training and education:** Foster an environment that encourages open dialogue, empathy, and respect for women within the organization.

3. **Implement communication guidelines:** Develop internal and external communication guidelines emphasizing transparency and respect.

Rebuilding the Brand

1. **Redefine the company's core values**, ensuring they align with the expectations and values of your customer base.

2. **Foster strategic partnerships.** Forge alliances with organizations that resonate with the target market, demonstrating a genuine commitment to positive change.

3. **Engage in meaningful corporate social responsibility initiatives** that address relevant issues. Focus on transparency and tangible impact to regain trust and demonstrate a genuine commitment to making a positive difference.

4. **Leverage brand ambassadorship**. Empower employees to participate in community service aligned with your company's values and amplify positive messages that restore the company's reputation.

5. **Maintain consistent and transparent communication.** Share updates on the progress, highlight positive changes and build a culture of open communication that fosters trust.

Damage Control Customize Exercise

Conduct a SWOT Analysis

a. **Strengths:** Identify and leverage the positive aspects of your organization to address the situation.
b. **Weaknesses:** Determine the vulnerabilities within your organization
c. **Opportunities:** Identify opportunities or positive actions to regain public trust.
d. **Threats:** Recognize the external challenges that may hinder the crisis resolution.

Make a Plan

a. **Acknowledge and understand.** Demonstrate a genuine understanding of the concerns and impact caused by the crisis.
b. **Apologize and distance.** Offer an apology to those affected by the situation and distance the organization from negative aspects.
c. **Outline specific corrective measures** you'll take to rectify the situation.
d. **Develop a comprehensive communication strategy** to address the crisis and rebuild trust.
e. **Determine how to engage** with customers, partners, or the public in a constructive and open dialogue to address their concerns.
f. **Implement initiatives** that promote ethical practices, demonstrate a commitment to positive change, and rebuild the organization's reputation.

Monitor and Respond

a. **Regularly evaluate** the progress of your crisis management plan and make necessary adjustments based on feedback, results, and changing circumstances.
b. **Establish a system** for gathering feedback, including social media, news outlets, and direct customer interactions.
c. **Promptly respond** to new developments or concerns, demonstrating your commitment to addressing the situation.
d. Once the crisis resolves, **review and identify** any areas for improvement to enhance your future strategies.

Learn and Preserve

a. **Study successful crisis management cases** in your relevant field.
b. **Analyze the strategies**, communication approaches, and actions.
c. **Extract and adapt** valuable lessons to fit your circumstances.
d. **Preserve documentation.** Keep comprehensive records of all commu-

nication, actions, and decisions to serve as a valuable resource for future reference, analysis, and learning.

Crisis management is an ongoing process. Stay vigilant, learn from each experience, and refine your strategies to build resilience.

Always thank and acknowledge any complaint – that's the Golden Rule!

Write a Letter of Apology

Dear (Name)

Thank you for raising your concerns about (name them) and their unintended effect on your (digestive system/human rights/religion).

While this was never our intention, we now see how you felt (hurt, excluded, insulted) by (our campaign/your treatment) and appreciate the time you have taken to deepen our understanding by bringing it to our attention so we can rectify matters from here on.

Your custom is important to us, and we are grateful for this opportunity to make amends.

We intend to (say what you intend to do), and we would like to invite you to (spend another night/discuss things in person/upgrade your ticket/upgrade the product/)

We thank you again for bringing this matter to our attention and look forward to regaining your trust and valued custom.

Yours,

Respond to a Scathing Venue Review

Always thank the reviewer for raising the issues. If possible, use them as a marketing opportunity to showcase your generosity. For example, if someone complains about the food, you could offer them a complimentary meal.

People will always read your response to a complaint. That's why addressing every issue head-on is essential. For example, a customer accuses a venue owner of giving her the cold shoulder.

More Harm Than Good
One-star rating

"My recent stay at Harmony Hills Retreat was a nightmare. My husband had paid in total but fell ill with a chest infection. We requested a reschedule, but Harmony Hills callously refused our plea. So, despite his condition, we arrived at the estate hoping for a pleasant stay.

It was not to be. The bitter cold chilled our bones when we stepped into our room. The staff promised to move us to a better suite. However, after we packed our bags, the receptionist told us the director had given the better suite to her friends, leaving us humiliated.

Harmony Hills refused us a refund, forcing us to stay another two days. My husband could not drive us home in his condition, so we shivered in our freezing room for the remainder of our stay.

Harmony Hills Retreat prioritizes money over compassion, and we suspect racial bias played a role in their mistreatment of us. Save yourselves the heartache we endured. Spread the word. Harmony Hills must learn from their mistakes."

Tata MaChance

Adapt the following response from Karen Bliss-Seeker, owner of Harmony Hills Retreat.

Dear Mrs. MaChance,

We welcome your valued feedback and extend our best wishes to you. Thank you for the chance to address some points from your review.

Regarding the room temperature, we sincerely apologize for any discomfort you experienced. We did our best to ensure a cozy stay by setting the air conditioning to 89° Fahrenheit: (32° Celsius). A welcome fire was lit in the grate using logs harvested from alien invasive trees on the property.

Promptly responding to your complaint, our staff discovered the air conditioning in your room had been adjusted to 64.4° Fahrenheit: (18° Celsius.) They reset it, rebuilt the fire, and provided an additional heater. After that, I regularly monitored your suite temperature from our online Ajax temperature detection app. I am happy to share the Ajax report that shows the temperature never dropped below 78.8° Fahrenheit (26° Celsius.).

Per the industry standard for last-minute cancellations due to illness, our terms and conditions are a fair 50% split of the cost between both parties. We were pleased to learn your husband was well enough to proceed with your stay.

You wanted to move to the Rock Pool Luxury Suite overlooking the river on Saturday morning. Regretfully, a regular client had booked it through me while I was driving, despite it showing as available on our online system. To soothe your evident frustration, our hostess offered you a full refund for the remaining nights of your stay (Saturday and Sunday) per our policy for situations involving guest disturbance. You turned down the refund and chose to stay for the additional two nights.

Our mission is to foster a welcoming and harmonious environment for every guest, so we are taken aback by your accusation of racism. Our diverse team works diligently to treat all our guests with the utmost respect and equality. After conducting a thorough investigation with the staff, we found no evidence to support your allegation, which you made public on various social media platforms.

As the owner of Harmony Hills Retreat, I must emphasize we take such accusations seriously. If these claims persist, we will take legal action to protect our business reputation. We hope to resolve this situation amicably but assure you we will not hesitate to defend ourselves if necessary.

Thank you once again for sharing your feedback. Should you wish to discuss this matter further, kindly contact us directly.

Sincerely,

Karen Bliss-Seeker, Owner, Harmony Hills Retreat

Turn Down a Proposal

On an individual level, if a company approaches you to work with them and your values don't align, here's a quick template for turning down proposals.

Dear (Client's name)

I sincerely appreciate the opportunity. Thank you for thinking of me. After careful consideration, I realized I could not dedicate time and attention to your project due to prior commitments and obligations.

I wish you the best of luck in finding a suitable partner for your project and continued success.

Sincerely,

Bonus Chapter

Hack the Art of Media Whispering

Are you tired of losing your message in the shuffle of an editor's inbox? Beat it by establishing a topical, irresistible treat!

Here's the thing. Journalists are a capricious bunch. Survival in the competitive, cut-throat media world is tough. A tsunami of press releases bombards their inboxes daily, so yours needs to stand out. Being on point is essential.

What do editors and journalists want? Something newsworthy, for starters. Rags-to-riches stories or unexpected life changes can work well. We appreciate PR professionals who research, respect our time, and provide relevant information.

Having toiled in the salt mines of mainstream media for decades, I've received more clunkers than a junk mail folder. I'm talking about those "no-go-nauts" that make editors hit the delete button faster than an I-know-the-answer contestant on *Who Wants To Be A Millionaire!*

I've seen everything from the spray-and-pray approach to high-visibility vest invitations, unsolicited advice, demands for upfront guarantees, and photographic frustrations. And I can tell you with certainty that the RUIN approach – Repetitive, Unsolicited, Irrelevant News – seldom facilitates the space you seek.

Below are some real-life examples of common tactics with a brief italicized explanation of why they annoy.

Don't Spray and Pray

Mass emailing hundreds of journalists at once is never a good idea. Neither are these opening lines.

Dear literary/travel/media contact/editor, hi, or hey, *Not addressed to me personally. Not my concern. *Delete without reading!**

Dear Cardine Hussy, *Um, it's Caroline Hurry, but whatever.*

"I hope you are well." *Miss me with your infuriating false bonhomie like you give a fandango about my health. You don't even know my name.*

Don't Assert Your Needs

We would need you to ... *You act like your needs interest me. Newsflash! They don't.*

Please read the attached press release and be so kind as to send us a copy of your article, visual or sound recording when it's aired or published. Thank you in advance for your cooperation. *Presumptuous much? Let me know how that works out for you! *Sender meets delete folder**

Don't Extend Late Invitations

Editors have a full schedule. Unless they're first-class air tickets to the city you've always wanted to see, last-minute high-visibility vest invitations are invariably as tempting as a fashion show featuring the latest hospital gowns.

"Space has made itself available at tomorrow's hot air balloon launch to view our city's extensive warren of parking garages from above." *Somebody bailed out of the basket. Call me high-maintenance, but I'm not your afterthought. Puncture that!"*

Don't Dress Puffy Marketing Fluff as News

Learn to understand the difference between a story and an advertisement. Changing an item on your lunch menu is newsworthy only if you're serving something exotic like crocodile belly or GM-free salmon.

If you start your release with "Exciting news from ...", ensure it *is* exciting. Also, unless this is a honeymoon familiarization trip to Seychelles, less is always more regarding instructions.

Don't Issue Instructions

"We suggest you interview Captain Incognito before publishing your article to grasp why he prefers not to reveal his true identity. *What about this: You stick to your mission. I'll stick to mine!*

"Be at The Underdog restaurant this Friday at 8 pm sharp – *This Friday evening? Sharp? Oh, my ribs!*

"– to hear Captain Incognito read extracts from his book *Two Sides*. Find signed copies for sale at the event. Feel free to use the following unembargoed print extract in your publication." *Gee, thanks!*

"In the wise words of Captain Incognito, "There are always two sides. *Nope. A quadrangle has four.*

"From any given point of view, there is the sable and the unseeable. *Does he mean the sable antelope, or has he misspelled seeable?* Just because the light at the end of the climate change tunnel is not seeable doesn't mean it's not there. *Waffle Quotient reached! Delete! Delete!*

Don't Send Irrelevant Unsolicited Pitches

Forget about placement if you don't find the most appropriate media outlet for your releases.

> "One bright spark spent me a press release for a dustbuster during my crime-beat days. It plopped into my inbox at 6 pm when I returned from a hectic day dealing with township murders. I binned it and blocked the sender from bothering me again."
>
> Janine Lazarus, media trainer and author

Don't Solicit Guarantees

"Thanks for accepting our invitation to introduce the esteemed Inn Sider's Pick to the broader discerning public.

"My client wants to know how you intend to write the review. What angle and tone will you take? *Aside from the oxymoronic 'broader discerning public,' how should I know when I've not seen the ISP? Remote viewing? Drone espionage?*

"My client has been talking to your publication's advertising manager. And? We don't share a duvet if that's what you're implying."

"He'd like to see our supplied images in the national supplement's center-spread." *That's sweet. I'd like to see a million copies of* Reign 16 Secrets *sold by May 2025.*

"Kindly fill in, sign, and return the attached forms of our requirements." *Sigh. Freelance journalists submit articles to commissioning editors. A response takes anything from 24 hours to never. If one door closes, they rap another media knocker. Their promise is as valid as a post-dated cheque from L. Ron Hubbard.*

Don't Call To Ask When It's 'Going In'

Don't. If you must pester a journalist, email them under the pretext of seeing if they need additional information. Get over it if there's still no response. Pieces get rejected all the time. It's nothing personal. Grow a thick skin and pitch at another publication.

> "Hats off to the Pee Aar who goes the extra mile, but going three rounds of email, WhatsApp, AND follow-up calls don't serve to remind, but to elevate your name to 'most annoying person ever.' Several more rounds of the same thing, for different events morph into this less-than-charitable thought: 'Her insecure tyrant of a boss has given her an attendance quota, poor thing. I'm not going to be the one who makes up 10.'
> Helen Grange, freelance journalist

Don't Express Disappointment

Worse than failing to thank a journalist or influencer for the publicity you received is telling them your client was disappointed.

"We note your contribution to the *Read and Weep Gazette*. My client is disappointed with your spin on the narrative we supplied concerning his philanthropy. He expected a more positive tone." *You're welcome. I'll be sure to file his grievances in my newly-plowed field of focaccia wheat.*

Photographic Frustrations

Context-free images are the bane of a journalist's life. And don't make us jump through hoops, either. "Download our image bank by requesting a password that changes every time you log in for your protection. It will take a few gigabits of your storage space." *That's not going to happen.*

"I have attached a few images for use in your article." *If a picture paints 1000 words, why were yours struck dumb? Who do you expect to write your captions? Me? Fine, but don't blame me if they're wrong!*

"Thanks for running the piece, but please, can you correct a mistake in the caption?" *No.*

7 Tips To Get Noticed

Target carefully: One size does not fit all when pitching. Familiarize yourself with the publication or website. Read back issues to determine what type of stories they cover. If you're promoting a memoir, the angle could be a unique aspect of your life story that readers can relate to or find inspiring And find out the editor's name.

Grab attention: Does your headline convey the essence of your piece? "Author writes a new memoir.' Dull. "Author Chronicles Her Journey From Lockdown to Sovereignty" is better.

Use a solid angle: Local publications often publish articles on personalities. Positioning yourself as an underdog or an upstart competing with multinationals might be newsworthy. Is your story entertaining? Is there a benefit to the community?

Punch up your introduction: Outline the relevance of your release in one brief straight-to-the-point paragraph.

Say it with stats: Sponsor or organize a study that produces newsworthy results. Relate your story to recent news. Example: "Research shows 85% of women suffer from low self-esteem. Documenting my struggles was a way of reaching out to others in the same boat."

Keep it brief: Aim for 300-500 words and avoid unnecessary details or fluff.

Explain who you are: Below the release, have you explained who you are to the editor? Remember to include up-to-date contact details – email, website address, or phone number. Include your business logo, if you have one, in the top right-hand corner of the page.

How to Woo the Media

Cultivating a huddle of journalists is crucial for any successful PR or marketing strategy. Fortunately, networking has never been easier. Charm, flattery, and persistence will win a journalist's heart. Like any seduction, the more foreplay you can put in, the greater your chances of success, so start the process early and approach from an indirect angle.

Being well-versed in their output helps you build a relationship, as journalists never tire of discussing the importance of their work. *Nothing* interests them more. The best media spadework is always intellectual with sycophantic leanings, so lavish your praise. Lay it on thick. You might think you're over-egging the custard. You're not.

Every journalist alive drinks in favorable feedback like a thirsty flower soaking up soft rain. That said, be judicious.

Avoid generic compliments like "I love your work" and instead reference a specific column, editorial, or feature. "So thought-provoking, and I especially liked what you said about women's rights or the topic *du jour*."

Six Media Matchmaking Tips

Create a media list. Start and maintain a database of media contacts - journalists who write about what you want to pitch. Use online newspapers that have emails of currently active journalists. Remember, all available media outlets – online blogs, websites, and email newsletters can be as good as national papers or consumer magazines. You need to ensure you send your press releases to the right person.

Set up Google alerts. You can use keywords to help you build information. To set up a <u>Google alert</u>, go to https://www.google.com/alerts. Enter the search query, such as your keywords or journalist names. Select the result type, frequency, and delivery method, then click "Create Alert."

Research their work on social media. Retweet their articles with salient comments or responses underpinning their ideas. Your interest builds a rapport based on mutual respect and intellectual curiosity. The trick is to be genuine and authentic. If you're using the journalist for their platform, they'll see through your approach in a trice.

Keep the channels you own up to date. One of the first things a journalist will do is Google you and check out your social media, such as LinkedIn or Twitter, so if they're not current, fix them. Set up your press kit on your website or author page with audio and video links. Include press clippings of publications and articles already published.

Give them something exclusive. For example, you can offer an advance copy of your book or an interview with you.

Insider tip: Start your note to the journalist with: "I'm not sure if this is your bag, but" to whet their appetite and lift any pressure.

> ***Hack:*** *Idioms: To hack it: (slang) to cope successfully with something. One who undertakes unpleasant tasks for money or reward; a hireling. A writer hired to produce routine or commercial writing – a slang word for a journalist.*
> Free Dictionary

Plant In The Soil

It's never too soon to sow genuine relationships devoid of Machiavellian motives, which any blogger or journo worth their salt will see through.

Hack Media Whispering With ChatGpt

Identify relevant contacts. Prompt: "Please suggest 10 practical ways to identify relevant media contacts in my niche and provide networking or exposure tips."

Craft Tailored Pitches Prompt: "How can ChatGPT help me tailor my pitches for each media contact based on their interests and previous work? Please provide research tools and personalized pitch templates."

Offer Insights and Expert Commentary. Prompt: "List 10 ways ChatGPT can help me provide relevant insights and unique perspectives to establish myself as a thought leader in my niche."

The Bonus Chapter was lifted from Write 6 Successful Self-Publishing Strategies,
Available here. https://mybook.to/UXfa

SCAN ME

LAYOUT LINKS

1. **A Collaborative Template**
   https://rb.gy/inn2v
   Or scan the QR code in the Share Chapter.

2. **Proof of Participation Template**
   https://tinyurl.com/4zr878vz
   Or scan the QR code in the Proof Chapter.

3. **Book Launch Template**
   https://tinyurl.com/ydjdw5
   Or scan the QR code in the Launch Chapter.

4. **Job Opportunities Template**
   https://tinyurl.com/rucbawa8
   Or scan the QR code in the Announce Chapter.

5. **Airline Feature Template**
   https://tinyurl.com/bdujavrs
   Or scan the QR code in the Showcase Chapter.

6. **Familiarization Tour Template**
   https://tinyurl.com/2p9yfp2n
   Or scan the QR code in the Host Chapter.

7. **Introductory Proposal Zoom Zelda**
   https://tinyurl.com/y5pzh8ce
   Or scan the QR code in the Introduce Chapter.

8. **Flaming Lorraine Template**

https://tinyurl.com/ke5dpnn9
Or scan the QR code in the Introduce Chapter.

9. **CEO Template**
https://bit.ly/3NGGiHE
Or scan the QR code in the Introduce Chapter.

More Useful Tools

- Answer the Public
  https://answerthepublic.com/
  Discover popular questions and topics related to your press release for potential angles.

- Bitly
  https://bitly.com/
  Shorten and track links to your press release for better analytics and monitoring.

- Calendly
  https://calendly.com/
  Schedule and manage appointments with journalists or media contacts for interviews or press briefings.

- Canva Infographic Maker
  https://www.canva.com/
  Design visually appealing infographics to present data or key information from your press release.

- Dropbox
  https://www.dropbox.com/
  Store and share press release documents, multimedia files, and press kits with media representatives.

- Facebook Pages
  https://www.facebook.com/pages/
  Create a dedicated page for your business or organization to share press releases and engage with your audience.

- Feedly
  https://feedly.com/
  A news aggregator that helps you stay up-to-date with the latest news and trends in your field of interest.

- Grammarly
  https://www.grammarly.com/
  A writing assistant that checks for grammar.

- Google Alerts
  https://www.google.com/alerts
  Set up alerts for relevant keywords to stay updated on media coverage and potential opportunities. Monitor online mentions of your press release, brand, or industry keywords.

- HARO (Help a Reporter Out)
  https://www.helpareporter.com/
  Respond to journalists' queries to provide expert insights or commentary and potentially secure media coverage.

- HubSpot CRM
  https://www.hubspot.com/products/crm
  Organize and manage your media contacts and track communication with journalists.

- Instagram
  https://www.instagram.com/
  Utilize visual storytelling to complement your press release and connect with journalists or media organizations.

- LinkedIn
  https://www.linkedin.com/
  Leverage the professional network to connect with journalists, share press releases, and establish industry relationships.

- Logo Creation
  Create five gorgeous high-resolution designs for free in six easy steps. Browse through hundreds of unique logo designs. Edit and customize the design you like to fit your brand. https://logo.com/how-it-works

- NewswireToday
  https://www.newswiretoday.com/
  NewswireToday offers a basic free option on its platform, focusing on technology, business, and industry news.

- Online PR News
  https://media.onlineprnews.com/
  They offer a freemium model, where the most basic press release package is free.

- Pew Research Center
  https://www.pewresearch.org/
  Provides tons of free info about our world. Enter whatever search terms you're looking for about demographics.

- Podbean
  https://www.podbean.com/
  Start a podcast to discuss press releases and industry news or provide expert insights to attract media attention.

- Podcaster Spotify
  https://podcasters.spotify.com/
  Easily record and distribute audio press releases or podcasts for media consumption.

- PRFree
  https://www.prfree.org/
  PRFree lets you create a free account to try out their press release distribution services to news outlets, search engines, and social media platforms.

- PRLog
  https://www.prlog.org/
  PRLog offers free press room hosting and discounted press release distribution to news websites, search engines, and social media platforms.

- Slack
  https://slack.com/
  Collaborate with team members or media contacts, share files, and discuss press release revisions.

- SoundCloud
  https://soundcloud.com/
  Share audio press releases, interviews, or industry insights to cater to a different media format.

- SurveyMonkey
  https://www.surveymonkey.com/
  Create surveys to gather feedback or conduct market research for your press release content or target audience.

- Twitter (X)
  https://twitter.com/
  Engage with journalists, industry influencers, and target media outlets to expand your press release's reach.

- URL Shortener
  https://tinyurl.com/app/
  Create shorter URLs

- Universal Links
  https://booklinker.com/
  Especially useful for books so that readers find it in their country.

- WordPress
  https://wordpress.com/
  Build a professional website or blog to showcase your press releases and attract media attention.

- Zoom
  https://zoom.us/download
  A platform for online video conferencing, webinars, and virtual meetings.

Afore Ye Go

If this book inspired creative flight
A quick rating or review would spark delight!
Thank you!

SCAN ME

About The Author

DRAWING ON HER EXTENSIVE background in journalism, editing, layout, and travel writing, Caroline Hurry provides a treasure trove of customizable press release texts and templates to empower aspiring authors, entrepreneurs, and professionals to make a splash in the media landscape.

Her other books include *Write, 6 Successful Self-Publishing Strategies on a Shoestring*, *Reign: 16 Secrets from 6 Queens to Rule Your World with Clarity, Connection & Sovereignty*, and *Flow 21 Secrets To Refresh Your Relationships*.

Website: www.carolinehurry.com

www.ingramcontent.com/pod-product-compliance
Lightning Source LLC
Chambersburg PA
CBHW072015290426
44109CB00018B/2242